TÊTE À TÊTE

PORTRAITS BY
HENRI CARTIER-BRESSON

INTRODUCTION BY
E.H. GOMBRICH

NATIONAL PORTRAIT GALLERY
LONDON

Design created and directed by Robert Delpire

This book was published to accompany the exhibition
Tête à Tête: Portraits by Henri Cartier-Bresson
held at the National Portrait Gallery, London,
from 20 February to 7 June 1998.
The exhibition will subsequently travel to the Ormeau Baths, Belfast;
the Scottish Gallery of Modern Art, Edinburgh;
the Walker Art Gallery, Liverpool;
the Royal Photographic Society, Bath;
the Laing Art Gallery, Newcastle upon Tyne,
and the Aberdeen Art Gallery.

The exhibition *Tête à Tête: Portraits by Henri Cartier-Bresson*
has been supported by British Telecommunications plc
as part of its Community Partnership Programme.

British Library Cataloguing-in-Publication Data
A catalogue record for this book is available from
the British Library

ISBN (paperback) 1 85514 247 3

Printed and bound in Germany by Steidl, Göttingen

FOREWORD

In 1998, Henri Cartier-Bresson will be 90. The greatest living photographer, he was trained as a painter and still spends much more of his life occupied by the craft of drawing than he does by the opening of the camera shutter. In fact, the first time he came to the National Portrait Gallery in connection with his exhibition, he had spent the morning quietly drawing in the National Gallery: watching, drawing, observing, while the crowds passed by, oblivious of the identity of the Frenchman on his shooting stick.

This was presumably part of his technique as a photographer: the capacity for invisibility; the eye for formal geometry; and the sensitivity to the circumstances of people who think themselves unobserved. He has not written much about his work, but in one brief sentence he has described the essence of his art as being the 'recognition, in a fraction of a second, of the significance of an event as well as of a precise organization of forms that give that event its proper expression'. It is, like his photographs, admirably succinct as an encapsulation of his technique, expressive, as well as accurate, in describing the combination of form and vision in the transformation of a small event into a memorable picture, framed, composed and recognized.

Throughout his career, portraits have been at the heart of Henri Cartier-Bresson's work. We therefore responded with huge enthusiasm when Eve Arnold first suggested we might be able to hold a celebratory exhibition of his portrait photographs. We are immensely grateful to her and to Magnum for all their help in connection with the exhibition, smoothing our path and enabling us to move the exhibition forward to the early part of 1998 in order to coincide with another Cartier-Bresson exhibition at the Hayward Gallery. We would particularly like to thank Brigitte Lardinois, the representative of Magnum, who has worked on all aspects of the organization of the exhibition; Agnès Sire, Magnum's curator in France; the Institut Français, who have organized a symposium with our education department; our friends and colleagues at the Hayward Gallery and the V&A, who have collaborated in making 1998 into a festival of Cartier-Bresson photography; and all those at Thames and Hudson, who have produced a catalogue at short notice. But most of all we would like to thank and pay homage to Henri Cartier-Bresson himself.

Charles Saumarez Smith
Director, National Portrait Gallery

THE MYSTERIOUS
ACHIEVEMENT OF LIKENESS

There is a *mystery* in the achievements of portrait likeness in what-
ever medium, whether you think of sculpture, graphic art, painting
or photography – a mystery, not to say a paradox, which is rarely suf-
ficiently appreciated.[1] After all, the impression of life usually rests on
movement. How, then, is it possible that there are images which give
us that feeling of standing face to face with a real person, masterpieces
of the art of portraiture which live on in our imagination, such as
Leonardo's *Mona Lisa*, or possibly the *Laughing Cavalier* of Frans Hals;
among those portraits of whom we know the sitters, Houdon's bust of
Voltaire comes to mind, and in this selection, the striking photograph
of Jean-Paul Sartre (Plate 47) taken in 1946, which, for many of us, has
fixed the image of the champion of Existentialism?

Indeed, here the mystery is compounded by yet another, because
after all, we have no way of knowing if these portraits had achieved a
convincing likeness. Would familiarity with her portrait have led us to
pick out Mona Lisa in the streets of Florence? And would we have recognized Jean-Paul Sartre or others of Cartier-Bresson's sitters at a party?
Maybe there is only one thing of which we can be absolutely sure: it is
that these men and women cannot have presented precisely the aspect
recorded in their portraits for more than a passing instant. The very
next moment they may have shifted their gaze, turned or tilted their
head, raised their eyebrows or lowered their lids, wrinkled their fore-
head or curled their lip, and each of these movements would radically
affect their expression.

Though language can describe some of the movements of the facial
muscles, our sensitivity to the slightest nuance far exceeds the power of
words. When we call the face 'the mirror of the soul' we mean that we

intuitively judge a person's character by the dominant facial expression. That is why Shakespeare's Hamlet is shocked to discover that 'one may smile, and smile, and be a villain'. He evidently forgot that there were many more kinds of smile than language can ever fully describe: the superior smile, the ironic smile, the joyful smile and the welcoming smile – their exact meaning depends on the rest of the configuration of the face, and even on the posture of the body; in this respect the effect of the interplay of muscles and features might be compared to the expressiveness of music, where by the shift of one semitone, the key turns from major to minor with its attendant change of mood. In both instances we are less aware of individual changes than of their resultant 'global' impression.

The most striking evidence for this global character of physiognomic likeness is offered by the successful caricature in which all the component features of the face are distorted, without affecting the resemblance of the whole.

I do not know if Cartier-Bresson has ever indulged in this wicked game, but his drawings in pencil, crayon and pen prove him to be an eager explorer of the varied landscape of the human face. As a photographer he is confined to a medium which objectively records and arrests the movements of the face – freezes them as it were – and this deadening accuracy surely renders the task of conveying a person's character more difficult than it is in other more flexible media.

To fully appreciate this difficulty, we must realize that any physiognomy, however crudely drawn, gives us the impression of a personality;[2] the reason why so many snapshots look to us unconvincing is precisely that they seem to represent not us, or a person we know; they look alien and unfamiliar. We dismiss a photograph as 'a poor likeness' when we do not recognize the expression as belonging to the repertoire of the person we know, not that the sitter is always a reliable judge in this matter – after all, looking into a mirror we are easily tempted to adjust our face to our taste. I am also aware that portraitists tend to

1 André Pieyre de Mandiargues, 1991

A.P de M
9.5.91
H.CB

à André L.
amilical
Henri 12.5.94
CB

dread the spouse who complains that there is 'something wrong about the mouth' in the portrait of her husband, which does not seem to be right for her – but here I am convinced that her reaction is based on a genuine response. The difficulty of catching the exact expression the sitter's intimates can accept as a likeness should not be underrated.

This problem inherent in achieving not *an* expression but the *intended* expression was known to artists throughout history. In fact, in the early fifteenth century, Leone Battista Alberti quite correctly wrote that it is not easy to distinguish in a painting a laughing from a weeping face. The development of this skill fills the history of art and has recently been described in a masterly book by Jennifer Montagu[3] which deals with one of the main landmarks in the conquest of the intended expression, a lecture by Charles Le Brun on Expression given at the French Academy in the seventeenth century.

The need to achieve a correct and legible expression arose from the demand of what was called History Painting – the illustration of events from the Bible, legend and ancient literature – a skill which culminated in the anecdotal subjects exhibited in the Salon. The special task of the genre of portraiture, however, was felt to lie elsewhere. From time immemorial the portrait was not so much intended to commemorate the private individual as the public figure. The seventeenth-century author Roger de Piles,[4] who had many sensible things to say about the art of the portrait painter, insisted that the chief task of the portraitist was to represent the role of his subject according to the conventions or rules of Decorum:

'… portraits … must seem to speak to us of themselves, and, as it were, to say to us – *Stop, take notice of me: I am that invincible king, surrounded with majesty—I am that valiant commander who struck terror every-where; or who, by my good conduct, have had such glorious success—I am that great minister, who knew all the springs of politicks—I am that magistrate of consummate wisdom and probity— I am that man of letters who is absorbed in the sciences. … I am that famous artisan, who was so singular in his profession, &c. And in women, the language ought to be … I am that high-spirited lady, whose noble manners command esteem, &c—I am that virtuous, courteous, and modest lady, &c.—I am that chearful lady, who delight in smiles and joy, &c.* And so of others. In a word, the attitudes are the language of portraits and the skilful painter ought to give great attention to them.'

These conventions dominated portraiture in the past. Thus, the aim of the Roman portrait was generally to express *gravitas* – the stern and serious mien of the *pater familias*; while a master of the Renaissance, such as Verrocchio, was able – in his equestrian statue of Colleoni – to monumentalize the fierce mien of the ideal *condottiere*, and in his busts of Florentine ladies, to embody the social ideal of the gracious smile which his pupil, Leonardo, then transfigured in the haunting expression of his *Mona Lisa*.

It is a well-known fact that the conventional ideals of decorum were taken up by the first photographers when the camera needed long exposures. The sitter had to keep still and generally assumed the familiar pose appropriate to his social role and dignity, and even in our century, the 'society photographer' continued to portray sitters in conformity with these stereotypes.

There is an amusing satirical passage in a novel by the American writer Allen Wheelis[5] that opens with a photographic session for a medical publication. As the committee members, whose portraits are to be taken, come in one by one, they are encouraged to take up the poses of their predecessors displayed in oil paintings on the wall; but the hero of the novel refuses to adopt the recommended posture, which he castigates as a lie: 'With the crossed legs, you claim repose, tranquillity. I am not fidgety and restless, jumping about on the edge of my chair, no idea what to do and where to go. Everything is under control. With the straight shoulders you say dignity, status, no matter what comes up, this guy has nothing to fear, is calmly certain

III Kem Payne, 1991

H.EB
2.87

of his worth and his ability. With the head turned sharply to the left, you understand that someone is claiming his attention – no doubt hundreds of people would like this guy's attention …', and he goes on to mock the pretence of the heavy tome held on the knees, and other attributes of the successful practitioner.

Wheelis's hero rebelled against the stuffy respectability of the establishment. Yet even if he had insisted on being photographed in shirt sleeves, with a cigarette in his mouth, he could not have avoided representing a recognizable type. My late friend the painter Sir William Coldstream, who was an excellent portrait painter and a great observer of men, told me that before he started on a portrait he did not tell the sitters – as some do – to 'be natural'; he told them to 'sit exactly as if you were having your portrait painted'. That, after all, was the reality they should not try to deny or evade. In this respect it could be claimed that most portraits must be seen as the result of collaboration, a compromise between the portraitist and the sitter. Almost any adult, in the presence of a camera, will become self-conscious and assume a pose. The more solemn the occasion, the greater will be the desire to *'far' bella figura'*.

Naturally, the brief exposure, the 'snapshot' that has become possible through the development of different lenses and films, has made it possible for the camera to catch the person unawares, and it is this possibility which has largely weaned us from the conventions of the society photographer. Yet it is also the snapshot that has alerted us to the perils of the frozen image, that so often presents us with a grimace, rather than a really living face. Many photographers have developed a routine of taking a large number of random shots from which they subsequently make a selection. As far as I know, Cartier-Bresson has always preferred to lie in wait for the telling moment.

The portrait painter, the graphic artist and the photographer must be aware of another decisive choice, even before the selection of the desired expression. I do not know if a code has ever been proposed for this special task, but it might start from the two basic aspects conventionally used in police records: the full face and the profile. These concern the permanent features of the head and, if it does not sound too childish, one might suggest that it be coded in terms of the direction in which the nose points, describing a quarter-circle from the frontal to the profile position. What is relevant here, as always, is the interplay between the structural and mobile parts of the face. Most noticeable of these, in the frontal view, are the eyes; in the profile, it is the position of the head on the neck.

Codes for postures of the body have in fact been developed by students of acting and of dancing, but there is one vital aspect that tends to elude them – what might be called the *'tonus'*, the degree of tension animating a movement, which decisively affects our response, both in life and in art.

These selected variables are merely outlined here to emphasize the outstanding range of positions explored and utilized in the art of Cartier-Bresson. The standard 'shot', the full frontal view with the eyes looking at the photographer, is rare. If he does use it, it is to record two opposing attitudes or expressions, largely distinguished by *tonus*: in the one, the sitter is engaging the attention of the photographer – even arguing with him, as in the case of John Berger (Plate 131) or Frank Horvat (Plate 17). But the frontal view can also indicate that the sitter, used to being photographed, has turned towards the camera and waits more or less passively for the click. The portrait of Stravinsky is a case in point (Plate 41), as is that of Duchamp (Plate 82), who sits back and watches the procedure with an air of ironic detachment. In one of the earlier photographs in this selection, that of Irène and Frédéric Joliot-Curie (Plate 27) of 1944, the couple conventionally face the camera, but their posture and their hands appear to reveal a profound embarrassment. The moving portrait of Rouault (Plate 14) in his old age, taken in the same year, has a similar air of resignation, much in contrast with that of Picasso (Plate 91), who faces the lens half naked, with extreme

V Yves Bonnefoy, 1979

HCB
3.77

11v93

self-confidence. Such self-confidence is also conveyed in the profile portrait of William Faulkner (Plate 10), while Max Ernst (Plate 76) and his wife are observed in pensive mood.

These two basic positions are experienced as relatively static – one could imagine the pose to have been held for some time, except where the movement of the eyes introduces a dynamic element. The photographer Martine Franck (Plate 18) is a telling example: she looks away while dreaming over her teacup. Even the portrait of Harold Macmillan (Plate 48), which comes closest to the observance of conventional decorum, is given a special twist by his sideways gaze.

The element of time becomes more prominent in cases where the sitters appear to be turning to look at the camera, as in the enchanting portrait of the pianist Hortense Cartier-Bresson (Plate 124), and that of the painter Avigdor Arikha (Plate 29), not to speak of that of Pierre Colle (Plate 123), whose upside-down head is shown emerging from a crumpled bed. While these scenarios may have been planned, there are also examples in this selection which show the photographer's luck and skill in catching a significant moment. I would put the portrait of Coco Chanel (Plate 35) among these; she seems to be engaged in lively conversation, and quite unaware of the camera; also that of the confident and cheerful Che Guevara (Plate 96).

I must leave it to the readers to continue the search for categories, or possibly to invent new ones; but one relevant variable still remains to be mentioned, since it is characteristic of all Cartier-Bresson's photographs: his attention to the composition of the image, which he never allows to be cut or cropped. It clearly makes a difference whether he shows us the head of Lucian Freud (Plate 79) far down in the right-hand corner, while the rest of the image is taken up by his easel, or whether the famous head of Camus (Plate 118) fills nearly the whole frame.

It is noteworthy, however, that Cartier-Bresson's drawings never rely on these compositional devices. Here his searching eye and hand concentrate on the isolated head and its expressive features.

These experiments take us to the final mystery of our response to the human face: the astonishing fact that, though we readily recognize our fellow creatures from the repertory of their gestures and movements, nothing more easily destroys or upsets our process of recognition than what we call 'disguise': go out and buy a conspicuous wig – preferably of a red colour and with long hair – and don it, and you will see with what astonishment you are greeted when you enter, so disguised, the next party you attend. How can this failure of recognition be explained? It appears that we must assume that our perception of people starts with categories. When a stranger comes into a room, we immediately register whether it is a man or a woman, the approximate age, and most of all, whether it is 'one of us' or an outsider. Every one of the symptoms of expression gains its validity and meaning only in this pre-established context; without such preconceptions we could never manage to interpret the infinite nuances of human appearance and their social significance. An initial mistake due to disguise will result in confusion upsetting the process of recognition that leads from the general to the particular in a smooth curve. Actors and producers on the stage make ample use of this tendency of the human mind to categorize people according to what they wear, according to their bearing and their role; a mask covering half the face will prevent recognition, and it is not without reason that medical textbooks create anonymity by obliterating the eyes of patients illustrated. This remarkable fact also has a bearing on our reaction to portraits – portraits of the past and portraits of the present. Because it turns out that, if you take the face out of its isolation and put it into the habit or the uniform of another age or calling, it looks entirely different. I have mentioned elsewhere[6] that members of the eighteenth-century Kit-Cat Club, displayed in the National Portrait Gallery, all look very much alike to us, transformed by their conspicuous wigs. Indeed, when we look at old family albums and come to members of earlier generations – the men with their bowler hats and their moustaches, the women with their high collars and

VII Ruta Sadoul, 1976

J.G.
4.9.94 HCB

tightly laced dresses – we begin to see them as types rather than as individuals, and find it hard to react to these images as we would to that of a contemporary. This observation has a bearing also on the exhibition of Cartier-Bresson's portraits of his contemporaries. How will they look, once their ways of dressing and behaving have receded into the past? We cannot tell; but since we are not put off by the attire worn by the sitters of Titian, Van Dyck, Rembrandt or Velázquez, we can be confident that they will retain that spark of life that only a master was able to impart to the photographic portrait.

E. H. Gombrich
December 1997

NOTES

1. I have discussed some of these issues in 'The Mask and the Face: the perception of physiognomic likeness in life and in art', *The Image and the Eye*, Phaidon (Oxford), 1982.

2. In my book *Art and Illusion*, Phaidon (London), 1960, I refer to this observation as 'Töpffer's law', after the Swiss painter Rodolphe Töpffer, inventor of the comic strip.

3. *The Expression of the Passions*, Yale University Press (Newhaven and London), 1994.

4. I quote from the English edition of 1743: *The Principles of Painting*, J. Osborn (London), pp. 168–179, translated from the French, published in 1708.

5. *The Scheme of Things*, A Helen & Kurt Wolf book, Harcourt Brace Jovanovich (New York and London), 1980, copyright Allen Wheelis.

6. *loc. cit.* under note 1.

VIII   Jean Genoud, 1994

PHOTO PORTRAITS

1 Ezra Pound, 1971

3 Glenn Seaborg, 1960

2 Lily Brik-Mayakovsky, 1954

4 Alfred Stieglitz, 1946

5 Iran, 1950

6 Robert Flaherty, 1946

7 The Pelopponese, Greece, 1953

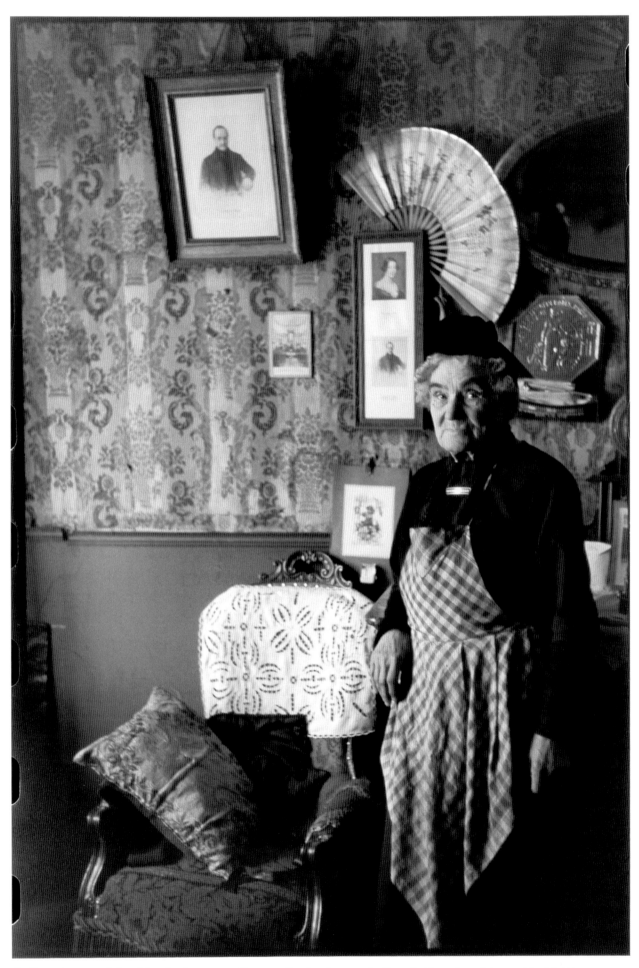

8 Concierge of the Musée Auguste Comte, Paris, formerly Sarah Bernhardt's maid, 1945

9 Kashmir, 1947

10 William Faulkner, 1947

11 Pablo Picasso, 1967

13 Alexander Calder, 1970

12 Edmund Wilson and his son, 1946

14 Georges Rouault, 1944

15 Jean Renoir, 1967

16 Arthur Miller, 1961

17 Frank Horvat, 1987

18 Martine Franck, 1975

19 Gjon Mili, 1958

21 Robert Oppenheimer, 1958

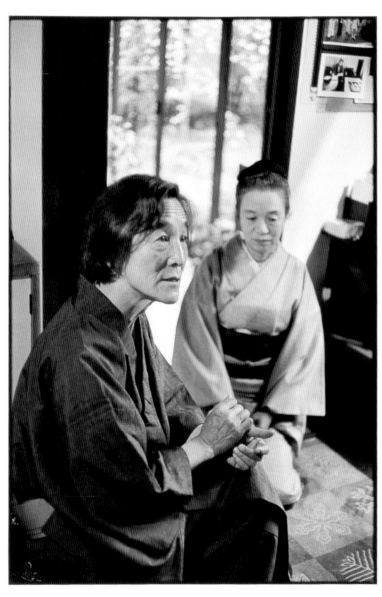

20 Hiroshi Hamaya and his wife, 1978

22 Pierre Bonnard, 1944

23 Henri Matisse, 1944

24 Truman Capote, 1947

25 Mary Meerson and Krishna Riboud, 1967

26 Mélanie Cartier-Bresson, 1978

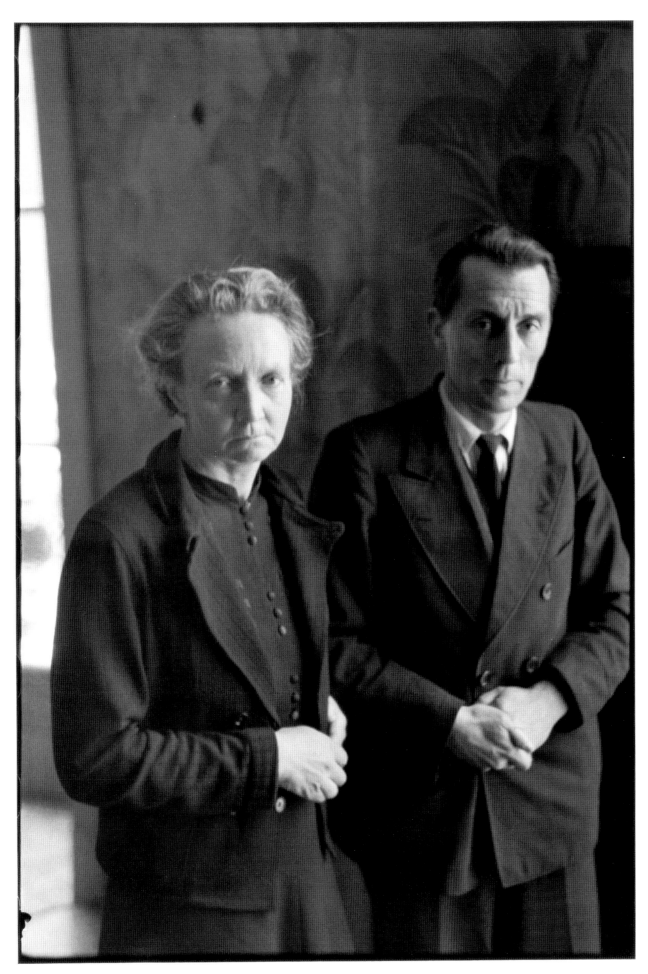

27 Irène and Frédéric Joliot-Curie, 1944

28 Barbara Hepworth, 1971

29 Avigdor Arikha, 1985

30 Calle Cuauhtemoeztin, Mexico, D.F., 1934

31 Tériade, 1951

32 Catherine Erhardy, 1987

33 Paul Léautaud, 1952

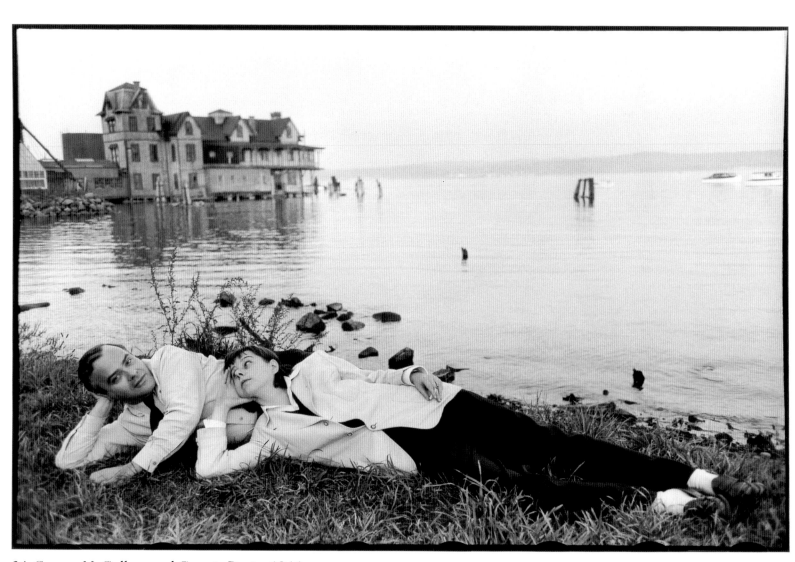

34 Carson McCullers and George Davis, 1946

36 Raymond Mason, 1993

35 Mademoiselle Chanel, 1964

37 Cordoba, Spain, 1933

38 Somerset Maugham, 1951

39 Martine Franck, 1986

40 Georges Braque, 1958

41 Igor Stravinsky, 1967

43 Louis Aragon, 1971

42 Nancy Cunard, 1956

44 Louis Kahn, 1960

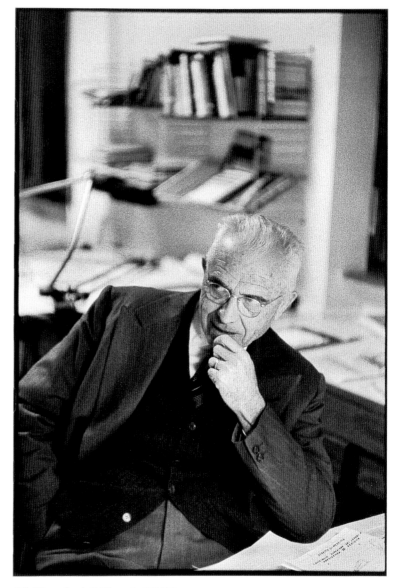

45 Pier Luigi Nervi, 1959

46 Paul Valéry, 1946

47 Jean-Paul Sartre, 1946

48 Harold Macmillan, 1967

50 Cecil Beaton, 1951

49 Lord Drogheda, 1967

51 Pierre Bonnard, 1944

52 Julien Gracq, 1984

53 Cyril Connolly, 1939

54 Robert Lowell, 1960

55 Giorgio de Chirico, 1968

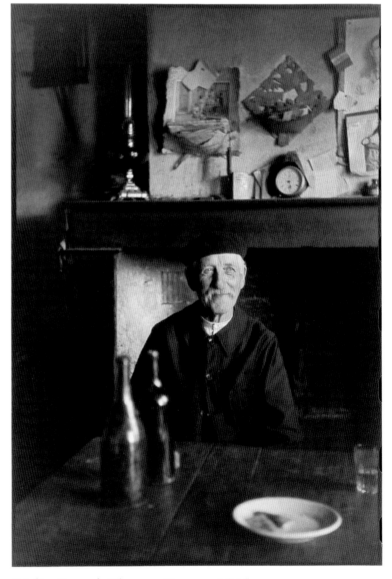

56 'Le Baron', Chouzy, France, 1945

57 André Pieyre de Mandiargues, 1991

58 Abbé Pierre, 1994

59 Susan Sontag, 1972

60 Carson McCullers, 1946

61 Alberto Giacometti, 1961

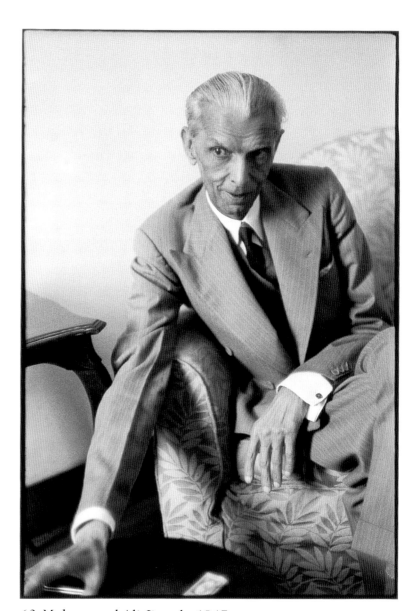

63 Mohammed Ali Jinnah, 1947

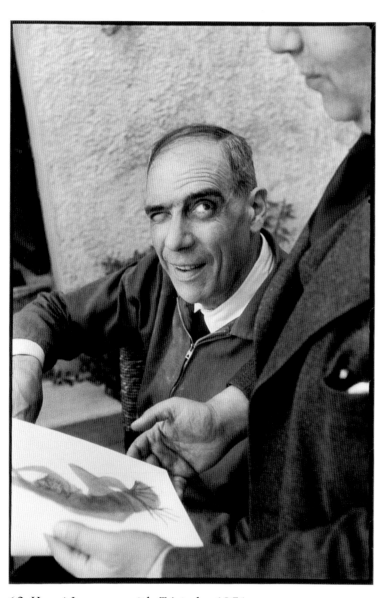

62 Henri Laurens with Tériade, 1951

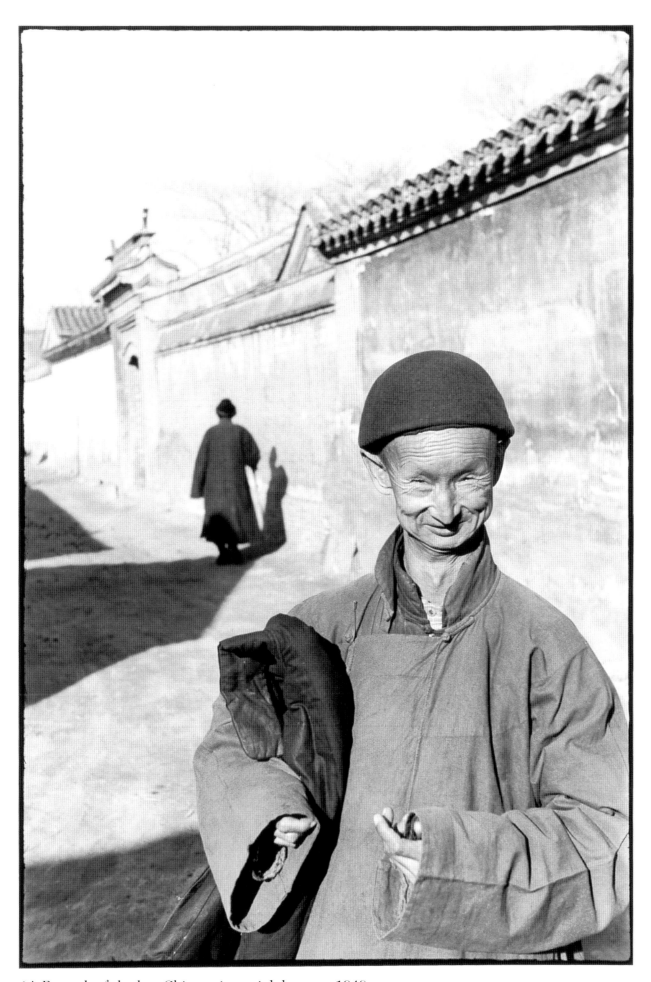

64 Eunuch of the last Chinese imperial dynasty, 1948

65 Koen Yamaguchi, 1965

66 Tenzin Gyatso, Fourteenth Dalai Lama, 1991

68 Georg Eisler, 1993

67 Max Ernst, 1955

69 Harold Pinter, 1971

70 Michael Brenson, 1981

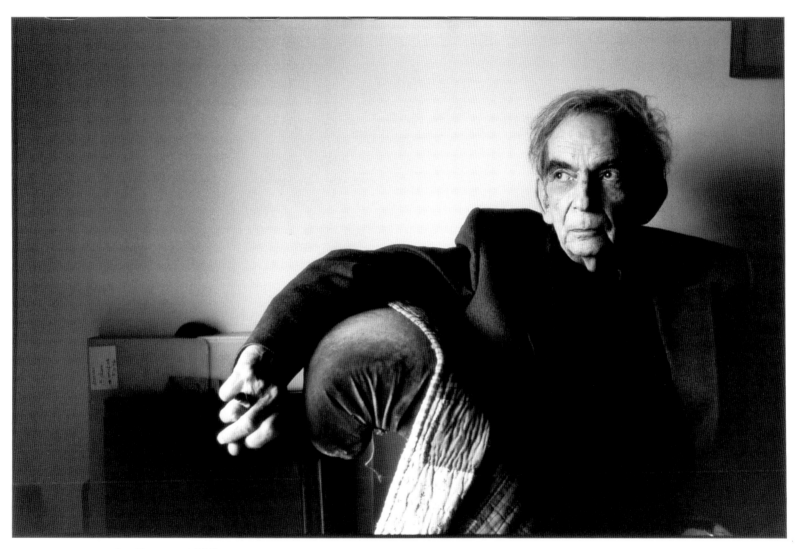

71 Louis-René des Forêts, 1995

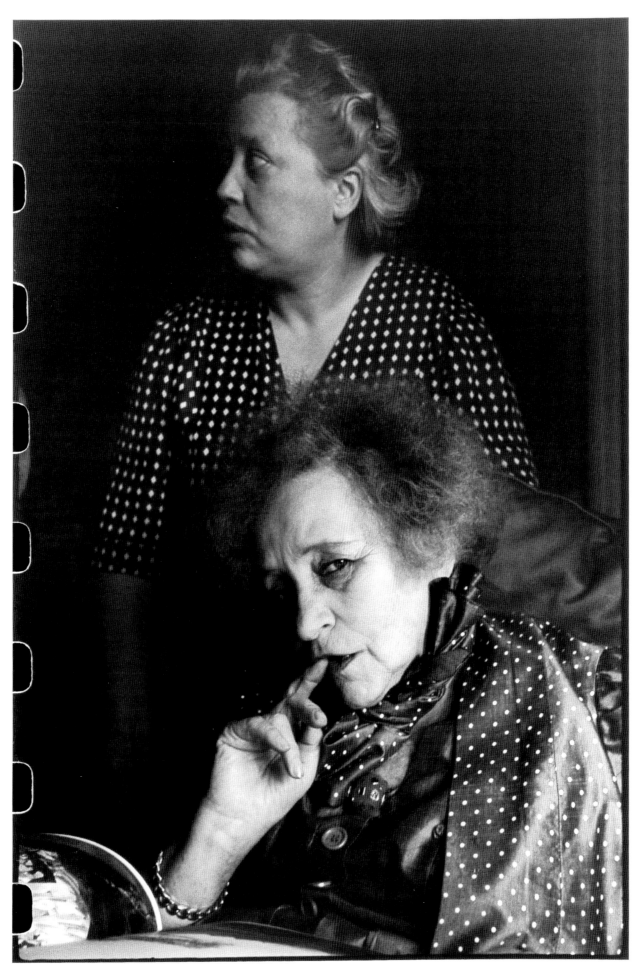

72 Colette and her companion Pauline, 1952

73 Sam Szafran, 1996

74 Igor Stravinsky, 1946

75 Francis Bacon, 1981

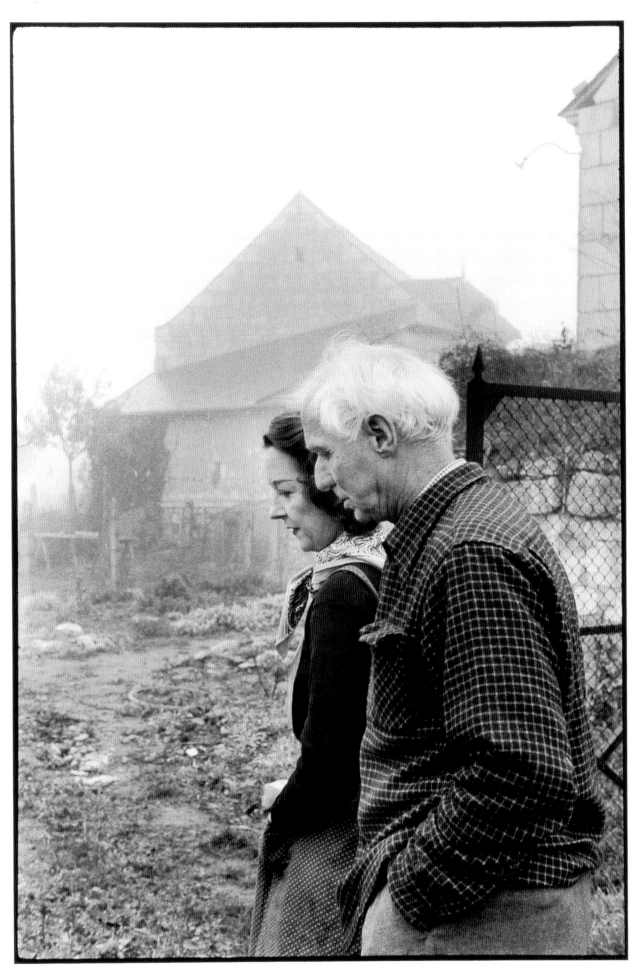

76 Max Ernst and his wife Dorothea Tanning, 1955

77 Katherine Anne Porter, 1946

78 Svetlana Beriosova, 1961

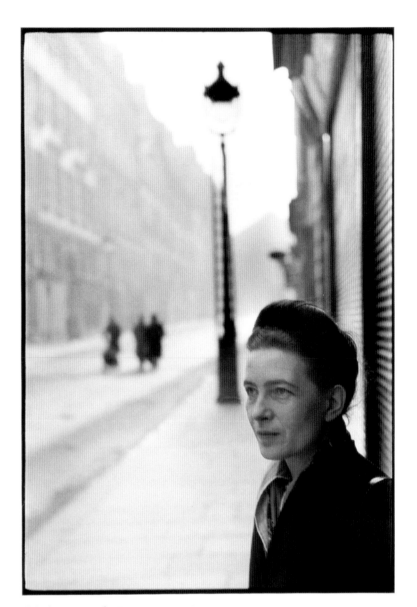

80 Simone de Beauvoir, 1947

79 Lucian Freud, 1997

81 André Breton, 1961

82 Marcel Duchamp, 1968

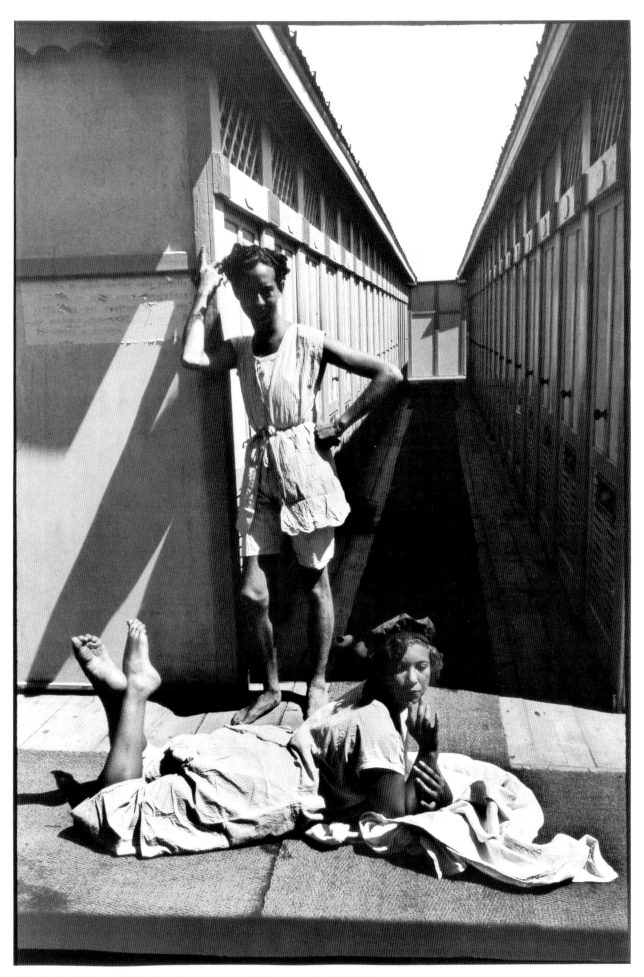

83 André Pieyre de Mandiargues and Léonor Fini, 1933

85 Pierre Josse, 1961

84 Igor Stravinsky, 1967

86 André Pieyre de Mandiargues, 1933

87 François Mauriac, 1952

88 Alexey Brodovitch, 1962

89 John Huston, 1946

90 Edith Piaf, 1946

91 Pablo Picasso, 1944

92 Ousmane Sow, 1995

93 Warsaw ghetto, 1931

94 Oaxaca, Mexico, 1934

95 Madurai, India, 1950

96 Che Guevara, 1963

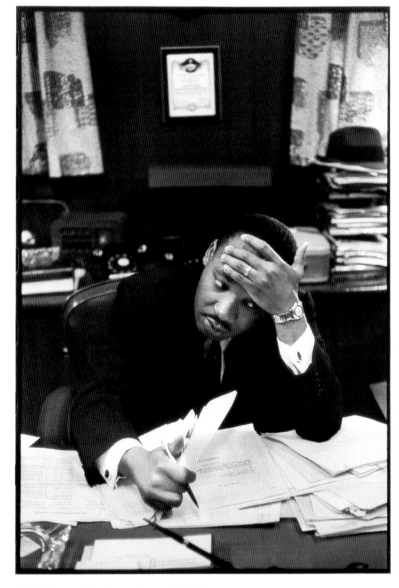

97 Martin Luther King, 1961

98 René Dumont, 1991

99 The brothers Joseph and Stuart Alsop, 1946

100 Tony Hancock, 1962

101 Marilyn Monroe, 1960

102 Ted Dexter, 1961

103 Robert Kennedy, 1962

104 Robert Doisneau, 1986

105 Saul Steinberg, 1946

107 Marc Chagall, 1964

106 José Bergamin, 1969

108 Eleanor Sears, 1962

109 Joe Liebling, 1960

110 Paul Scofield, 1971

111 Dominique de Ménil, 1960

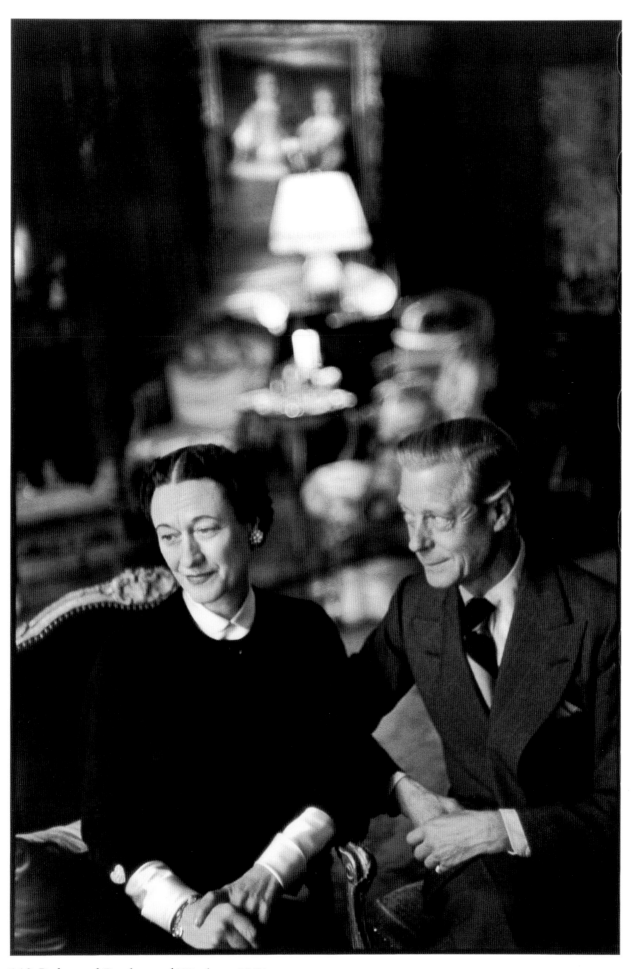

112 Duke and Duchess of Windsor, 1951

113 Zoltán Kodály and his wife, 1964

114 Christian Bérard, 1946

115 René Char, 1977

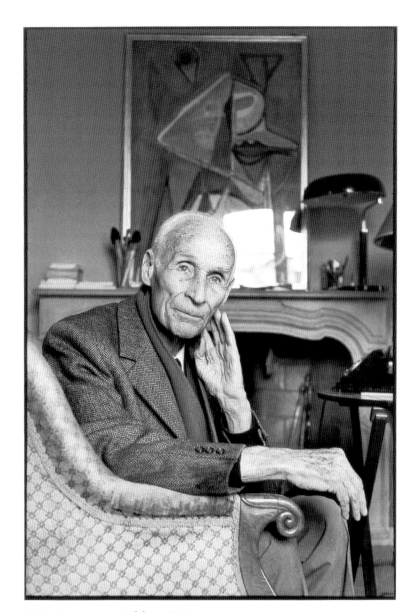

117 Bram van Velde, 1977

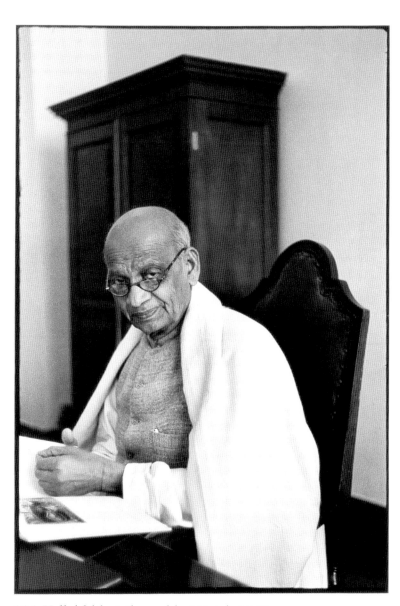

116 Vallabhbhai Jhaverbhai Patel, 1948

118 Albert Camus, 1947

119 Alexander Schneider, 1960

120 Jeanne Lanvin, 1945

121 Samuel Beckett, 1964

123 Pierre Colle, 1932

122 Hungary, 1964

124 Hortense Cartier-Bresson, 1979

125 Jakarta, Indonesia, 1949

126 Krishna Roy between Rita and Tara Pandit, 1946

127 Joe the trumpeter and May, 1935

128 Balthus, 1990

129 Elisabeth Chojnacka, 1991

130 Jean Genet, 1963

131 John Berger, 1994

132 Alberto Giacometti, 1961

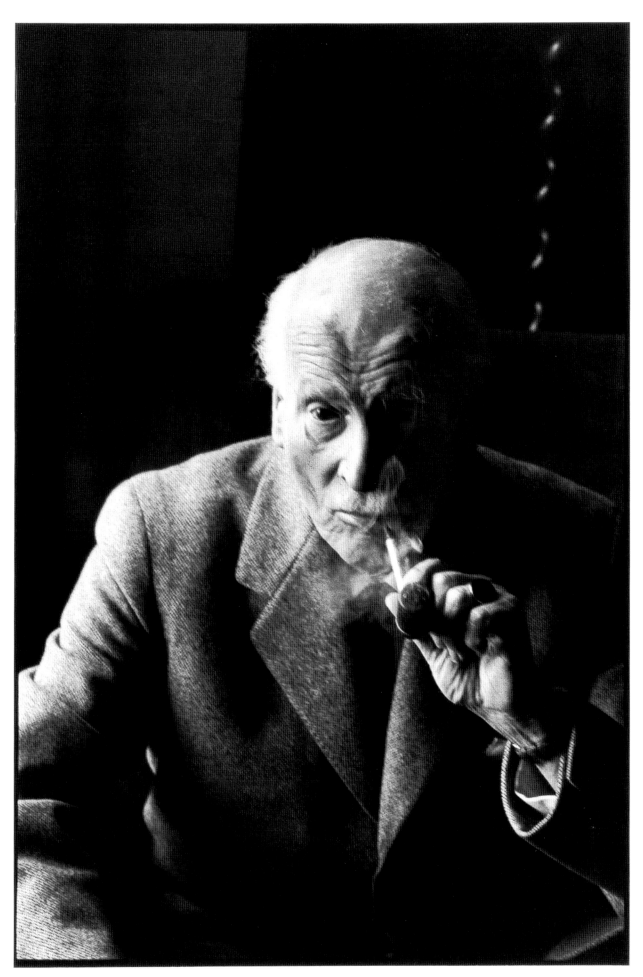

133 Carl Gustav Jung, 1959

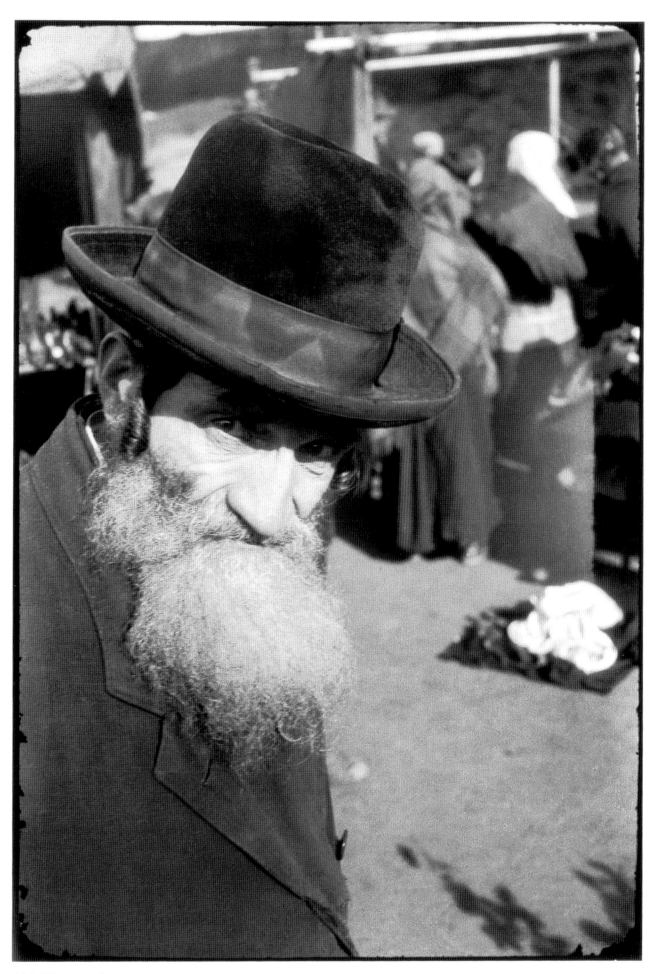

134 Warsaw ghetto, 1931

INDEX OF NAMES

Arabic numerals refer to plate numbers,
Roman numerals to the drawings

Henri Cartier-Bresson would like especially to thank Daniel Mordac and his team at Pictorial Service and Marie-Pierre Giffey at Magnum Paris.